OVERCOMING SPIRITUAL
STRONGHOLDS SERIES

Overcoming
the Spirit of
Poverty

by
Rick Joyner

MorningStar Publications

A DIVISION OF MORNINGSTAR FELLOWSHIP CHURCH

375 Star Light Drive, Fort Mill, SC 29715

www.MorningStarMinistries.org

Overcoming the Spirit of Poverty
by Rick Joyner
Copyright ©1996
Eighth Printing, 2008

Published by MorningStar Publications,
a Division of MorningStar Fellowship Church
375 Star Light Drive, Fort Mill, SC 29715
www.MorningStarMinistries.org
1-800-542-0278

International Standard Book Number: 978-1-878327-55-0

Overcoming the Spirit of Poverty

Table of Contents

Introduction

The spirit of poverty is one of the most powerful and deadly strongholds Satan uses to keep the world in bondage. Every church and every believer must fight and overcome this enemy in order to walk in the purposes for which they are called. This stronghold is one of the enemy's most successful weapons against us. But by overcoming it we will gain a place of spiritual authority from which we can be used to meet some of the world's most pressing needs. Wherever this stronghold is overthrown, it is like casting off the darkness of the most terrible spiritual winter and seeing the world blossom into spring again.

When we think of poverty, we usually think of money or economics, but the spirit of poverty may or may not have anything to do with these. *The spirit of poverty is a stronghold established for the purpose of keeping us from walking in the fulness of the victory gained for us at the cross, or the blessings of our inheritance in Christ.* This can relate to everything from the quality of our marriages to the anointing we have for ministry, as well as any other resources that we need for what we have been called to do.

AN rules where there is two things present! ;
DARKNESS & Ignorance
Truth of God Breaks His power!

The goal of the spirit of poverty is not just to keep things from us, but to keep us from the will of God. To do this, Satan may even give us great riches, but our lives will nevertheless be just as empty and full of worries as if we were destitute.

The first step toward defeating the works of darkness is to understand them. We must then apply what God has said in relation to them. Satan is called the prince of darkness because darkness is his domain. His main strategy is to keep us from seeing the light of God's Word. Therefore, whenever the light of understanding shines on something, his authority over it is broken.

Because Satan can only rule where there is darkness, or ignorance of the truth of God, truth breaks his power. This is why the Lord said, **"and you shall know the truth, and the truth shall make you free" (John 8:32)**. Both the Lord Jesus and the church are called **"the light of the world" (see John 8:12; Matthew 5:14)**. Jesus came to **"destroy the works of the devil" (see I John 3:8),** and He did this by shining light into the darkness. When we walk in the light as He did, we will also destroy the enemy's works.

The Lord has given us divinely powerful weapons for the destruction of strongholds (see II Corinthians 10:4). Strongholds are maintained by what the Scriptures call principalities. We can cast out demons, but we must wrestle against principalities (see Ephesians 6:12). Wrestling is the closest form of combat, and it is one in which we seek to displace our foe. Principalities will not flee just because we command them to. We must push them out by walking in the light that exposes them. Truth, spoken by the anointing, is the most powerful weapon there is, and we have been entrusted with it.

Our goal for being free from the spirit of poverty is not just to have things that we need or want, but that we can do the will of God without hindrance from either physical or spiritual depravity. When the world witnesses our freedom, it will start asking for the answers that we have. When we are free from the yoke of the spirit of poverty, our freedom will be manifested in the natural as well as the spiritual. Spiritual authority will always have dominion in the natural realm as well, just as the Lord's spiritual authority was manifested by His healing the sick, raising the dead, and even multiplying food.

One evidence that we have been truly freed from the yoke of the spirit of poverty is financial independence. Financial independence does not necessarily mean that we are rich or can buy anything we want. It does mean that we are free of every financial yoke so that we only make decisions based on what the will of the Lord is and not on how much money we have or do not have. It may be the will of God for us to have a lot or to have a little. Like the Apostle Paul, we must be content if we are either abased or abounding, as long as it is the will of God for us. That is the key phrase: *if it is the will of God for us.* We do not want to be either abased or abounding if it is not His will. The key for liberation from any evil stronghold in our lives is to know God's will.

It is important for the church to be prepared to handle unprecedented wealth. There are a number of prophetic Scriptures which indicate that the wealth of the nations will be brought into the church. This will be a great opportunity *for* the advancement of the kingdom. But it will come as a result *of* the advancement of the kingdom. We must remember that some of the greatest tests at the end of this age will be economic. That is why the mark of the beast is an economic mark, which determines whether we can buy, sell, or trade. If we are not freed from the yoke of the spirit of poverty when we receive wealth it will only further corrupt us.

In the end, when the greatest economic trials are coming upon the world, the faithful will be standing on a Rock that cannot be shaken. That is why many are going through economic trials now. All of them are meant to free us. They are tests, which are for the purpose of promotion. It is now time to pass them so we can go on to the better things.

It is imperative that we set a goal for being financially independent because that is His will for all of His children. It is not His will for any of His children to be bound by the yokes of this world. There is a clear, biblical strategy that will both get us there and keep us there—if we follow it faithfully.

We must seek financial independence but always keep in mind that it is a means and not the end in itself. To be financially independent without knowing our purpose in God would be like getting all dressed up with no place to go. Getting free of this stronghold is for the purpose of enabling us to do His will. Seeing that purpose is part of the motivation that it will take to be faithful to His Word. I have therefore concluded this booklet with a section on achieving our purposes.

Rick Joyner

Part I

Get Out of Jail Free!

One of the most basic conflicts between the kingdom of God and this present age is that the latter is built on slavery. The Lord came to set men free. Everything that Satan does is intended to increase the yoke of bondage upon us. Everything that the Lord does is intended to set us free. As we proceed toward the end of the age, the differences between these two kingdoms will become increasingly pronounced.

How do we get free to live in the kingdom of God? This is the quest of every believer. Once our lives are firmly established in the kingdom, we must seek to tear down the strongholds of the enemy and set his captives free. In our battle, we must always remember that the conflict is between slavery and freedom. If you belong to Christ Jesus, you are called to be free!

It was for freedom that Christ set us free; therefore keep standing firm and do not be subject again to a yoke of slavery (Galatians 5:1).

The Lord purchased us with His own blood. We belong to the King of kings. He has called us to be sons of God and joint heirs with Him. We are called to represent His kingdom as ambassadors, walking as members of the highest nobility, royalty of the highest order, and God's own family. To do this, we must be free from the yokes of this present evil age and carry only His yoke.

> **"Come to Me, all who are weary and heavy-laden, and I will give you rest.**

> **"Take My yoke upon you, and learn from Me, for I am gentle and humble in heart; and you shall find rest for your souls.**

> **"For My yoke is easy, and My load is light" (Matthew 11:28-30).**

Yokes represent bondage. There are yokes of bondage through which men are kept in darkness and oppression. These yokes usually appear to be a form of freedom, but result in the most terrible burdens. In contrast, the Lord's yoke appears at first to be bondage, but results in the greatest freedom we can ever know.

We will all carry someone's yoke—either the yokes of this present evil age or the yoke of the Lord. If we are to carry the Lord's yoke, we must cast off every yoke of the enemy. We cannot serve two masters. The one whose yoke we carry will be the one we serve and represent in this world. We can make every claim to be a Christian, but if we live our lives according to the ways of this present evil age, we are serving the powers of evil.

> You adulteresses, do you not know that friendship with the world is hostility toward God? Therefore whoever wishes to be a friend of the world makes himself an enemy of God.

> Or do you think that the Scripture speaks to no purpose: "He jealously desires the Spirit which He has made to dwell in us"?

> But He gives a greater grace. Therefore it says, "GOD IS OPPOSED TO THE PROUD, BUT GIVES GRACE TO THE HUMBLE."

> Submit therefore to God. Resist the devil and he will flee from you.

> Draw near to God and He will draw near to you. Cleanse your hands, you sinners; and purify your hearts, you double-minded (James 4:4-8).

There can be no compromise. If we are yoked to the world, we are serving the world. If we are yoked to the Lord, we will serve Him only. As we proceed to the end of this age, the differences are going to become more pronounced and the battle between the two kingdoms more fierce. All of this is happening for the purpose of setting us free!

All that happens will result in the Lord having a bride that is prepared for Him without spot or blemish.

The Scriptures are clear that great troubles are coming upon the world at the end of this age. Even if we believe we will be raptured before the **"great tribulation" (see Matthew 24:21),** which the Lord said was just **"the beginning of birth pangs" (see Matthew 24:8),** it is clear that we must be prepared for difficulties. Our preparation for difficulties is to seek first the kingdom, live in the kingdom, and always represent the kingdom of God, which is simply to obey the King.

If we are faithful to this, we do not have to fear these difficulties whether or not we believe that we will go through the tribulation. The kingdom of God cannot be shaken, and if we have built our lives upon it we cannot be shaken either. Every difficulty that comes upon us now is to help build our lives on the kingdom of God.

—Difficulty —
—Trial —Crisis

For it is time for judgment to begin with the household of God (see I Peter 4:17).

When we hear the word **"judgment,"** we often equate it with destruction caused by the Lord's ultimate wrath. If we read the Scriptures in the languages in which they were originally written, we would not feel this way.

The Greek word that is translated **"judgment"** in this text is *krisis*, the word from which we derive our English word *crisis*. A definition of crisis is "the point in a disease or trauma when it is determined if the patient will live or die." This Scripture could thus have been translated, "It is time for a crisis to begin with the household of God." The implication is that the church will go through a crisis before the world does. God allows this so that when the world is going through a crisis, we will be on solid ground.

This is why James wrote the following:

> **My brethren, count it all joy when you fall into various trials,**
>
> **knowing that the testing of your faith produces patience.**
>
> **But let patience have its perfect work, that you may be perfect and complete, lacking nothing (James 1:2-4 NKJV).**

Here we see that trials produce patience, which leads to our perfection so that we will not lack anything. That is true biblical prosperity.

"The earth is the LORD's, and all it contains, the world, and those who dwell in it" (Psalm 24:1). Even though it is presently subject to bondage because of the Fall, the Lord is going to take this world back. We have been called to be a part of His invasion force, but we can only be on one side in this battle. We must now get free of every yoke of the enemy that causes us in any way to compromise the ways of the kingdom of God. The trials we are now going through are all meant to help us do this.

The Lord is not the least bit worried about the economy or any other human problems. We are called to be seated with Him in the heavenly places (see Ephesians 2:6). Our Lord will never lack the resources to do what He wants to do. Neither will we ever lack the resources to do what He wants us to do.

The Mark of the Beast and the Mark of God

Because **"the love of money is the root of all evil" (see I Timothy 6:10 KJV)**, money tests some of the ultimate issues of the human heart. Idolatry is one of the ultimate offenses against God. Money is one of the primary idols in the world today. An idol is not just something that people fear or worship, but what they put their trust in. Money in itself is not evil, but how we relate to it can be a factor that determines the entire course of our lives for good or evil.

Many sincere Christians still have idolatry in their hearts in relation to money because they trust more in their jobs or bank accounts than they do in the Lord. Because we know that one of the ultimate tests that comes upon the people living in the last days will revolve around the **"mark of the beast," (see Revelation 16:2),** which is an economic mark that determines whether we can buy, sell, or trade under his system, it is imperative that we confront this in our lives now.

In Revelation 7:1-3, we see that four angels are sent to hold back the four winds of the earth until the bondslaves of God have been marked on their foreheads. Believers have spent a great amount of time trying to figure out how this mark of the beast will come so they will not be fooled by it, but there has been almost no attention given to how we take the mark of God. The only way we will not take the mark of the beast, regardless of whether we know what it is or not, is to have the mark of God. If we are marked by God, we will never have to fear taking the enemy's mark.

These angels will hold back the winds of the earth, which are the violent forces that are destined to sweep the earth, until the bondservants are sealed. The key to understanding this seal of God is to understand the bondservant, just as the key to understanding the mark of the beast is to understand that those who take the mark serve the beast.

When Slavery Is Freedom

It is obvious that not all believers are bondservants. Many really do come to an understanding of the sacrifice of Jesus for their sins, but they still go on living their lives for themselves. We were the slaves of sin and were purchased by the cross. If we are Christ's, we are no longer our own, for we belong to Him. A bondslave does not live for himself, but for his master. This commitment is not just an intellectual agreement with certain biblical principles; it is the commitment to a radical lifestyle of obedience.

A bondservant does not have any money or time of his own, and he cannot freely spend what he has been entrusted with since it is not his. Even his family belongs to his master. To voluntarily become a slave is the ultimate commitment that can be made in this world, which is what it really means to embrace the cross. Those who are truly bondslaves are the ones who will receive His mark.

Even though the Lord purchased us with His blood, He will not force anyone to be His bondservant. In Scripture, a bondservant was one who was able to go free, but loved his master so much that he chose to be his slave for the rest of his life. We, too, are free to choose whether or not we will be bondservants. God allows us to choose whether or not we will serve Him because freedom is required for true worship and true obedience from the heart. There can be no obedience from the heart unless there is the freedom to disobey.

16

The reason He put the Tree of the Knowledge of Good and Evil in the Garden was to give man the freedom to choose whom he would serve. This was not to cause man to fall, but rather so that man could prove his devotion. If all the Lord had wanted was obedience, He would have done better to have just created computers and programed them to worship Him. Would this kind of worship be acceptable to anyone, much less our glorious Creator?

We are free to go on living for ourselves, but it is the ultimate folly. We must know the Lord as our Source and keep our trust in Him. The key to our survival in this time is being a bondslave. Every master is obligated to provide for his slaves, and we have the most dependable Master of all. He will take care of His own.

Being a bondservant of the Lord is to become His slave, but it is also the greatest freedom we can ever know in this life. When we are united with Him by taking His yoke, we die to this world just as He did. When we are truly dead to the world, there is nothing the world can do to us. It is impossible for a dead man to fear, to be offended, or to feel remorse because he loses some of his possessions. To the degree that we fear the loss of our possessions or positions, that is probably the degree to which we are still

17

not dead to these things. The enemy uses fear to bind us just as the Lord uses faith to set us free.

When we are dead to this world but alive to Christ, all of the treasures of this earth seem petty and insignificant because we have Him. When we are seated with the King of kings on His throne, what pull can any earthly position have for us? This does not mean that we do not have a genuine care for our jobs or ministries here. We care for them because they have been entrusted to us by Him, and we engage in them as worship unto Him. If our positions here are taken from us, we are still seated with Him, and we will worship Him in whatever way He calls us to next. We are His slaves, and we must be content with whatever job He gives to us.

When Christ is our life, trust, and the true desire of our hearts, He can trust us with the earthly possessions and positions that we are called to rule over. But if He is not our life, trust, and the desire of our hearts, our possessions and positions will inevitably rule over us. Whoever or whatever rules over us is in fact our lord. We are entering a time when the lordship of Jesus must be more than a doctrine—it must be a profound and continuing reality in our lives. Then we will be free indeed. When we are fully yoked to Him, having cast off all the yokes of this present evil age, He will then be free to trust us with the unlimited resources of His kingdom.

18

PART II

Receiving the Wealth
of the Nations

A law of physics states that energy is never destroyed, but simply changes forms. The same is true of wealth; it is never destroyed, but often changes hands. Even during the Great Depression, wealth was not destroyed, but was transferred to those who were in a position to take advantage of the time. Those who were in this position were not in debt and had cash readily available. Businesses were bought for as little as 10 percent of their value. Land was bought for as little as a dollar an acre. The wealth was taken from those who had overextended themselves with debt and was received by those who had the wisdom to live within their means.

We are heading for an even greater economic upheaval than the Depression. It may come this year or it may come in ten years or more—but it will come. Those who are not prepared for it will be devastated. Those who are prepared will take advantage of the time and receive authority over unprecedented wealth. We are being prepared for this by the problems He is allowing us to go through now. The psalmist wisely exhorted:

Therefore, let everyone who is godly pray to Thee in a time when Thou mayest be found; surely in a flood of great waters they shall not reach him (Psalm 32:6).

The Lord is allowing us to go through troubles now that are meant to drive us to higher ground. Even if we have been faithful in all things, sometimes the Lord still allows us to go through troubles, just as He did Joseph, so He can trust us with even more of His abundance.

Like Joseph, we are being prepared to properly manage the abundance we receive so it can save lives during the times of famine that are coming. The Lord wants His people prepared to use the circumstances that are coming for the sake of His gospel, not just so we can get rich. One fundamental flaw that will keep us bound by the spirit of poverty is selfishness. When it comes to the Lord trusting us with more resources, motives are crucial.

The Lord is right now preparing His people for what is about to come. He has been warning His church for over twenty-five years to get out of debt. He has given us plenty of time to do it. However, because the expected catastrophic economic problems have taken so long to come, many have disregarded the warning. There is still time to repent and get our houses in order, but we must not delay.

Those who are obedient will have nothing to fear from what is coming but can look forward to a godly prosperity in the midst of famine. Those who continue in disobedience will pay a terrible price for it.

Don't Go Back to Jail

We were bought with the highest price that could be paid—the blood of the Lamb. Because **"the borrower becomes the lender's slave" (see Proverbs 22:7),** when we go into debt we sell ourselves to become the slave of another. If we belong to Christ we are not our own to sell. When we go into debt we are actually selling that which belongs to God. YES!

Does this mean we should never go into debt for anything? In principle this is true. However, we must understand that we do not live under the law—there is a difference between principles and laws. Laws cannot be broken, but there are exceptions to principles. This does not mean we can just disregard principles any time we want to. It means that we need to hear very clearly from the Lord to do so.

For example, I know some people who years ago felt they should not go into debt for a house, even though the mortgage was less than the lease payments and the house was in an appreciating market. At the time I felt that this debt was permissible, but they disagreed. Now these people are still leasing, with payments that are much higher than they were then. They could have now owned the house outright with its value more than quadrupled.

This still does not necessarily mean they should have bought the house, especially if their consciences would not permit them to. Many believe that **"owe no man any thing, but to love one another" (see Romans 13:8 KJV)** is an emphatic command that we cannot compromise. However, if it were an emphatic commandment, why did He chastise the foolish servant in the Parable of the Talents for not at least getting interest for His money (see Matthew 25:24-28)? Would the Lord encourage us to loan money at interest if it were a sin to borrow under any circumstance?

In the Old Covenant, the Israelites were commanded not to loan their money at interest to their brethren, but this had nothing to do with loaning at interest to others, which is why the Jews have been the most outstanding bankers in history (see Deutoronomy 23:19-20). Even so, as a principle (not a law), it is better not to go into debt for any reason without a clear directive from the Lord. We must get out of debt and stay out of debt except when we are clearly permitted to do otherwise for a season.

PART III

Christian Economics 101:

The Art of Stewardship

Christian economics is the art of good stewardship in obedience to the simple biblical procedures which the Lord has laid out for us. Stewardship is the emphasis of a substantial portion of the Bible, and it must become a major emphasis for our time.

As the Lord made clear in the Parable of the Talents (see Matthew 25:14-30), we must seek to use everything the Lord has entrusted to us in the most profitable way. It is right that we give more emphasis to our spiritual gifts than our natural resources. However, what is often overlooked in this parable is that the kind of talents the Lord was talking about was money. In Bible times, talents were a form of currency. Certainly we must not exclude the literal interpretation of this parable as well. Recorded in Luke 16:9-13, we have another related exhortation from the Lord:

> **"And I say to you, make friends for yourselves by means of the mammon of unrighteousness; that when it fails, they may receive you into the eternal dwellings.**

"He who is faithful in a very little thing is faithful also in much; and he who is unrighteous in a very little thing is unrighteous also in much.

"If therefore you have not been faithful in the use of unrighteous mammon, who will entrust the true riches to you?

"And if you have not been faithful in the use of that which is another's, who will give you that which is your own?

"No servant can serve two masters; for either he will hate the one, and love the other, or else he will hold to one, and despise the other. You cannot serve God and mammon."

The statement that we **"cannot serve God and mammon"** means we cannot combine the motive of serving God with the motive of making money. There is abundant evidence throughout history that the love of money will quickly corrupt a ministry. But we must not exclude the first part of the Lord's exhortation in this text: **"Make friends for yourselves by means of the mammon of unrighteousness."** In this, He is not telling us to be friends with the mammon, but to use mammon to make friends.

The Lord also makes it clear in this text that we must learn to be faithful with worldly goods before we can be entrusted with the true riches of the kingdom. Learning to properly handle unrighteous mammon while maintaining a right spirit is important for every Christian. We must learn to do this now. Since the ultimate conflict between the spirit of this world and the kingdom of God will revolve around economics and the ability **"to buy or to sell" (see Revelation 13:17),** this exhortation is even more critical and timely.

Check the Source

If prosperity is your primary goal, then you will serve the one who gives it to you. Just as Satan promised Jesus, if you will bow down to worship Satan, which is to live by his ways, he will give you everything that God has promised you (see Matthew 4:9). Jesus had already been promised all of the kingdoms of the world. Satan's temptation was to take the easy way, to seek to attain that promise without going to the cross. Satan will promise you everything that God wants to give you, and he will also show you a quicker and easier way to attain it. Satan is the present ruler of this age, and he can do it.

Taking the mark of the beast is not the sin that brings the judgment. The sin is to *worship* the beast. The mark is simply evidence that

25

one has been worshiping him. Will we escape judgment if we refuse to take a mark but then go on living our lives according to the ways of the beast? Of course not. Rather than being so concerned about the mark, we should be concerned about how we may be serving the ways of the beast.

The mark of the beast is probably far more subtle than many have been led to believe, just as the mark of God is not literal, but spiritual. Even if the beast's mark is literal, the only way that we will not take it is to have the mark of God's bondservants. This is the reason why the events of these times have been restrained by the four angels who are holding back the winds. God is right now marking those who are true bondservants.

The Yoke of the Beast

Debt is probably the main reason why Christians today are not free to respond to the call of God in their lives. When there is a call to do anything, from entering the full-time ministry to going on a mission trip, if our main consideration is whether we can afford it, it is an indication that our financial condition rules us more than the will of God does. It is a revelation of just how much we have built our lives upon the foundations of this present age, rather than hearing and obeying the Word of the Lord.

This must change and change quickly, for all of us. Our situations can change! The Lord is going to provide a way of escape for those who will be obedient. Regardless of how disobedient or how foolish we have been, or how bad our situations are now, if we repent the Lord will deliver us. Our God really is all-powerful. When He helps there is no limit to what can be done. When His people are trapped with the hordes of the enemy bearing down on them, He delights in doing some of His greatest miracles.

If we call upon the Lord in faith, He will part an ocean to get us free if He has to. However, true faith begins with true repentance for whatever we have been doing that is wrong. Repentance does not just mean that we are sorry, but that we also turned away from our wicked ways. As C.S. Lewis pointed out, once we miss a turn and start down the wrong road, it will never become the right road. The only way we can get back on the right road is to go back to where we missed the turn. The Lord does not want to deliver us just to have us slip right back into bondage because we did not change our ways. Therefore, true repentance is evidence of the true faith which compels Him to respond.

Attaining Financial Independence

There is a clear biblical procedure for getting out of debt, for staying out of debt, and for becoming financially independent.

The biblical definition for financial independence is being in the place where you never have to make a decision based on financial considerations, but simply on the revealed will of God. This is the condition in which every Christian should live. This should be our first and most important financial goal.

Regardless of how bad our present financial condition is, there is a very simple biblical formula that will provide a sure way of escape:

REPENTANCE + OBEDIENCE = FREEDOM

We must start by recognizing any ways in which we have departed from the clear mandates of Scripture and then begin to obey the clear and simple biblical instructions for financial management. If we do, we will escape our present situation and begin to live a life of freedom that is better than we have ever dreamed.

Wrong Move

Most of us think that the way out of our situation is to make more money. That is almost never the answer to financial problems and can even make matters worse. God's plan for financial independence does not require us to make more money, and He is probably not going to give us a revelation so that we can win the lottery. We may not think that there is any other way, but there is.

If God can multiply the bread and the fish, He can cause whatever we are now making to go just as far as He wants it to. All we must do is obey the simple and clear instructions that He gave us in the Scriptures for managing what He entrusts to us.

When we have proven our trustworthiness with what we now have, He promises to give us more to manage. Remember, He is giving it to us to manage, not to have. We are His bondservants, and we therefore do not have anything of our own. It is all His, and we must not spend it on ourselves unless He gives us permission. We must always maintain this perspective if we are to avoid falling back into bondage.

Before Going On

Before we continue with the theme of Christian economics, we need to address an important and related issue. The church is still wounded in many areas that Satan intended to cripple her. These are the very areas where she must have power for what is to come, so she must be healed in these areas now.

PART IV

Repentance 101: Receiving Kingdom Authority

Remember that the formula for financial independence is: REPENTANCE+OBEDIENCE= FREEDOM. This section deals with the repentance that most of us will have to do before we can even understand what we are required to obey.

Becoming Vessels of Power

It is by the Lord's stripes that we are healed. In the very place where He was wounded, He received the power for healing. The same is true for us. In the very places that the enemy is allowed to strike us, once we are healed, we will receive authority for healing in those same areas. For example, a person who has suffered abuse becomes sensitive to others who have had the same problems, and their compassion for the abused can release the Lord's healing power.

True spiritual authority is founded on compassion. When the Lord saw that the people were like sheep without a shepherd, He became their Shepherd. Compassion releases the power of God. Every wound we have suffered in our lives was for the purpose of making us sensitive and compassionate toward others who have suffered in the same way so that He can release His healing power through us.

Almost every person on the planet has been held in bondage to the financial yokes of this world and/or has received financial wounds from all manner of theft and deceit. The Lord is going to use His church to break the enemy's financial power over multitudes and set them free. He has allowed the enemy to wound His church in this area in order to make her sensitive and compassionate so we can help set others free.

Before we can be used to heal others, we must be healed of our own wounds. One of the requirements for being a priest was that he could not have scabs (see Leviticus 21:20). A scab is the result of an unhealed wound. Those who have scabs are so overly sensitive in that area that you cannot touch them. Likewise, our unhealed wounds keep people from getting close to us in those areas. This keeps us from being able to intercede for those who need our ministry. Spiritual scabs, therefore, can disqualify us from our most important ministries.

Even though we can receive the power of healing in the same places where we were wounded, our wounds must be healed first. Scars may remain, which may continue to be a little sensitive, but not so sensitive that no one can get close to us. The sensitivity of scars is different from that of scabs. Scars keep us just sensitive enough to help us discern the wounds in others that have not yet been healed.

The Way of Escape

The first principle to getting out of our present financial bondage is not to get, but to give. If you cringed at that statement, it is the evidence of a wound that must be healed. Our foe has the wisdom of thousands of years of ruling over his dark domain, and he has wisely attacked the most important issues with his biggest weapons. He has taken some of the most important words in Scripture, such as "holiness," "submission," and "giving," and made them repulsive even to Christians. Yet these truths will be recovered by those who overcome.

It is true that the church has been raped. Rape is the ultimate violation of a person. Rape is therefore one of the most difficult traumas for a person to recover from. The church has been raped repeatedly by hype, manipulation, and those with a control spirit. If the Lord could have prevented this, why didn't He? What loving father would allow his daughter to be raped if he could prevent it? Our heavenly Father allowed His Son to be crucified unjustly because He has a higher purpose. His goal is ultimately to use His Son, working through His church, to remove all rape from the earth for all time.

We must understand that nothing bad has ever happened to us that the Lord has not allowed. He does love us, even more than we love our own children. He has not let anything happen to us that was not for our good and for the higher good of His whole creation. We must stop sulking over our wounds and understand that they were allowed so we could receive authority over the very one who wounded us and be the vessels of healing for other victims. This is why the Apostle Paul wrote the following:

> **Now I rejoice in my sufferings for your sake, and in my flesh I do my share on behalf of His body (which is the church) in filling up that which is lacking in Christ's afflictions (Colossians 1:24).**

This Scripture does not imply that the work of Christ was not complete. The word translated **"lacking"** here could have been translated "left behind." The implication is that He allows us to go through sufferings for the same reasons that He did, with the

33

exception of the propitiation. Our sufferings are also meant to help release redemptive authority into the world. That is why when defending his authority Paul pointed to his tribulations. All suffering that a believer endures has a redemptive purpose.

Even though the Lord allowed His own bride to be raped, He is going to do a great miracle. He is going to take the church that has been raped repeatedly, and at other times has played the harlot, and make her into a pure, chaste virgin again. In the very place where she was the most severely abused, she will be healed and will then be given the power to heal others.

The Lord is also going to raise up a last-day ministry that will never again rape His bride. They will be spiritual eunuchs for the sake of the kingdom. A eunuch cannot even have a desire for the bride. His whole purpose is to prepare the bride for the king, and his satisfaction comes from seeing the king's satisfaction. That will be the nature of the ministry that is coming. They will not be in ministry to take from the church, but to serve her.

There will be a people raised up before the end that follows the Lord fully. However, it is to be expected that it will take the church a long time to trust them, or anyone, after the past abuses. Many believers have responded to the financial abuses by refusing to give any more. This is understandable, but until they are free from this attitude, they will likely stay in financial bondage. Giving is fundamental to Christianity. Giving our money is one of the primary ways we are freed from its powers of idolatry. Therefore, these issues must be addressed without compromise for the sake of those who have been so wounded.

Today we can be free from all of our spiritual wounds and never look back on them. They need not affect the rest of our lives. The way of escape is the cross, which is manifested by forgiveness.

The two most powerful beings in the universe are trying to kill us—God and Satan. One of them is going to do it. Who do you want it to be? We can hang on to our wounds and the injustices committed against us and let Satan kill us. Or we can go to the cross, forgive and be forgiven, and let God kill us. This is a choice we must all make, and there are benefits to each. Let's look at each one.

If we let Satan kill us, it will be a slower death. We can also keep our bitterness and resentment. We might also have the satisfaction of getting even with those who abused us, and sometimes that feels really good.

If we let the Lord kill us, there are some downsides that we need to consider. He will do it very fast, but because it is so fast, there can be some very intense pain. The cross hurts! We will also have to give up our plans to retaliate against our abusers. We will even have to give up the desire to see God judge them. We must completely forgive and actually pray for those who persecute us. We will even have to love our enemies! He will not let us off the cross until we, like Him, say, **"Father, forgive them"** (see Luke 23:34). One of the greatest problems is that our forgiveness and love may even cause some of our enemies to come to the Lord, and we will have to live with them forever!

The benefits of letting the Lord kill us are rather appealing though—peace that no person or circumstance can ever steal from us, love that feels much better than resentment, and, best of all, eternal life with Him, with our Father and all of His angels, our loved ones, and even with some of our former enemies.

There is only one way we can know the power of the resurrection, and that is to die. We are called to die daily, but we are also promised that if we do, we will experience resurrection power in our daily lives. We all want to go to heaven, but before we do, the Lord wants us to bring some heaven to earth. We have been given the highest calling a person can have—we have been called to be ambassadors of His kingdom. That means that we are to be walking demonstrations of the kingdom of God. Are we?

The Last Battle

The Lord said that **"the harvest is the end of the age" (see Matthew 13:39).** The harvest is the reaping of everything that has been sown, both the good and the evil. We also see in the Bible that the tares are gathered first (see Matthew 13:30). The Lord starts the judgment with His own house because He cannot judge the world if His own people are living in the same evil conditions. There will be a distinction between His people and the world when the judgments come, but it will be because His people are different.

The issues here are much greater than whether you get out from under financial pressures or get out of debt altogether. This is not just about financial independence. It is about destroying our idols and becoming true worshipers of God—those who worship Him in Spirit and truth. It is having a solid foundation upon which to confront the greatest darkness of our time.

YES!

We simply cannot live by the standards, desires, lusts, and ways of this present evil age and the kingdom of God at the same time. This does not mean that we cannot have a house, car, or television set. It does mean that we will only have that which we have permission to have. It also means that we **"do all things for the sake of the gospel" (see I Corinthians 9:23)** and that our first consideration in making any major decision will be to determine our Master's will. We must also start by doing now what is clearly written in His Word.

Part V

Repentance 102:
The Most Deadly Enemy

The devil has many titles in Scripture, but his most effective guise has unquestionably been **"the accuser of our brethren" (see Revelation 12:10).** He seems to know better than the church that when we come into unity, he is doomed. Therefore, his number one strategy against us is to keep us divided. His most successful strategy for this has been to get us to accuse one another. He does this by releasing a critical spirit, which releases criticism. Criticism is also the number one way by which we release the spirit of poverty into our own lives.

The Lord made some remarkable promises in Isaiah 58:8-9, if we would remove this critical spirit from our midst:

> **Then your light will break out like the dawn, and your recovery will speedily spring forth; and your righteousness will go before you; and the glory of the LORD will be your rear guard.**

> **Then you will call, and the LORD will answer; you will cry, and He will say, "Here I am." IF**

you remove the yoke from your midst, the pointing of the finger, and speaking wickedness. *Critical spirit*

Here we are promised that if we remove the yoke of criticism from our midst (which is portrayed as **"the pointing of the finger, and speaking wickedness"**), our light will break out, our healing will come speedily, the glory of the Lord will follow us, and He will answer our prayers. There is possibly nothing that can so radically change the church, and the lives of individual believers, than having the critical spirit removed from our midst.

The best way to remove it is to have our criticisms changed into intercession. The Lord ever lives to intercede, while the devil lives to accuse. If we would stop siding with the devil and see people through the Lord's eyes, our first response to seeing something wrong with another person would not be to accuse them, but to intercede for them. How quickly would we all be changed by just this one thing? How much more unity and therefore more power would there be in the church? The Lord said that it would result in light, healing, glory, and answered prayer. What more do we need?

This text makes it clear that our addiction to criticism is the main reason why there is so little light, so little healing, so little of the glory of the Lord, and so little answered prayer in the church today. Criticism is probably the biggest open door that the spirit of poverty has into the lives of believers because criticism is one of the ultimate manifestations of pride. Whenever we criticize someone else, we are assuming that we are superior to them. Pride brings that which any rational human being should fear the most—God's resistance. **"God resists the proud, but gives grace to the humble" (see James 4:6 NKJV).** We would be better off having all the demons in hell resisting us rather than God!

Whom Are We Criticizing?

When we criticize another Christian, we are actually saying that God's workmanship does not meet our standards and that we could do it better. When we criticize someone else's children, who takes offense? Their parents! This is no less true with God. When we criticize one of His people, we are actually judging Him. When we criticize one of His leaders, we are really judging His leadership.

Such grumbling and complaining is the same problem that kept the first generation of the children of Israel from possessing their Promised Land. Their grumbling caused them to spend their entire lives wandering in dry places. This is the chief reason why many Christians stay in such dryness and do not walk in the promises of God. James warned us:

Do not speak against one another, brethren. He who speaks against a brother, or judges his brother, speaks against the law, and judges the law; but if you judge the law, you are not a doer of the law, but a judge of it.

There is only one Lawgiver and Judge, the One who is able to save and to destroy; [when we judge the law, we judge the Lawgiver]; but who are you who judge your neighbor? (James 4:11-12)

When we **"point the finger"** to criticize, we yoke ourselves.

"Judge not, that you be not judged.

"For with what judgment you judge, you will be judged; and with the measure you use, it will be measured back to you" (Matthew 7:1-2 NKJV).

I once visited a state that was under one of the most powerful spirits of poverty that I have witnessed in this country. This was remarkable because it is a state of great beauty and natural resources, with talented and resourceful people, but a spirit of poverty was on almost everyone. Another characteristic that stood out was that almost everyone I met there seemed to uncontrollably scorn and criticize anyone who was prosperous or powerful.

With every pastor of a small church that I met (and almost all of the churches in this state were very small), the conversation would inevitably turn to criticizing "megachurches" and "megaministries," which these people obviously thought were the reason for many of their own problems. What made this even sadder was that many of these small-church pastors were called to walk in much more authority than the leaders of the large churches or ministries that they criticized. When I prayed for them, the Lord showed me that their judgments and criticisms of others had restrained His grace in their own lives.

Many pastors yoke themselves and their congregations to financial poverty by criticizing how other churches or ministries take up offerings or solicit donations. Because of their judgments on others, they cannot even take up a biblical offering without feeling guilty. Again, as the text in Isaiah 58 states, the primary reason for the darkness, unanswered prayer, and lack of healing and the glory of God in our churches is not the devil or other outside problems—it is our own critical spirit.

Of the many people I have met with exceptional spiritual giftings but with the lack of spiritual fruit, this has always been a prevailing characteristic in their lives. They had judged and criticized the ministries of others who were gaining influence and had thereby disqualified themselves from being able to receive more. Our criticisms will bring us to poverty. **"Death and life are in the power of the tongue, and those who love it will eat its fruit" (Proverbs 18:21).**

Solomon observed:

> **But the path of the just is like the shining sun, that shines ever brighter unto the perfect day.**
>
> **The way of the wicked is like darkness; they do not know what makes them stumble (Proverbs 4:18-19 NKJV).**

If we are walking in righteousness, we will be walking in increasing light. Those who stumble around in the dark seldom know the reason for that darkness, or they would not be in it. However, a critical person is a prideful person who will therefore be critical of everyone but himself because he cannot see his own sin. As the Lord stated, he is so busy looking for specks in the eyes of his brothers that he cannot see the big log in his own eye, which is the reason for his blindness (see Matthew 7:3-5).

44

We are all saved by grace. We will need all of the grace we can get in order to make it through this life. If we want to receive grace, we had better learn to give grace because we are going to reap what we sow. If we expect to receive mercy, we must start sowing mercy. Most of us are going to need all the mercy we can get. The Lord sternly warned:

> "You have heard that it was said to those of old, 'You shall not murder, and whoever murders will be in danger of the judgment.'

> "But I say to you that whoever is angry with his brother without a cause shall be in danger of the judgment. And whoever says to his brother, 'Raca!' [empty head] shall be in danger of the council. But whoever says, 'You fool!' shall be in danger of hell fire.

> "Therefore if you bring your gift to the altar, and there remember that your brother has something against you,

> leave your gift there before the altar, and go your way. First be reconciled to your brother, and then come and offer your gift.

> "Agree with your adversary quickly, while you are on the way with him, lest your adversary

deliver you to the judge, the judge hand you over to the officer, and you be thrown into prison (bondage).

"Assuredly, I say to you, you will by no means get out of there till you have paid the last penny" (Matthew 5:21-26 NKJV).

It is clear by this warning that if we have been guilty of slandering a brother, we should forget about our offerings to the Lord until we have been reconciled to our brother. The Lord links these together because we often think that our sacrifices and offerings can compensate for such sins, but they never will. We will stay in the prisons we make for ourselves with our judgments until we have paid the last cent, or until we are reconciled to the brother we slandered.

If we will remove this terrible yoke from our midst, the Lord promises in Isaiah:

"Then you will call, and the LORD will answer; you will cry, and He will say, Here I am....

"And the LORD will continually guide you, and satisfy your desire in scorched places, and give strength to your bones; and you will be like a watered garden, and like a spring of water whose waters do not fail.

"And those from among you will rebuild the ancient ruins; you will raise up the age-old foundations; and you will be called the repairer of the breach, the restorer of the streets in which to dwell" (see Isaiah 58:9, 11-12).

PART VI

Christian Economics 102: Obedience

As mentioned, our formula for financial independence is REPENTANCE+OBEDIENCE= FREEDOM. In this part we are going to address obedience a little more deeply.

Two more important biblical texts for the church today are found in Haggai 1 and Malachi 3. Let's prayerfully consider them:

> "Thus says the LORD of hosts, 'This people says, "The time has not come, even the time for the house of the LORD to be rebuilt."'"
>
> Then the word of the LORD came by Haggai the prophet saying,
>
> "Is it time for you yourselves to dwell in your paneled houses while this house lies desolate?"
>
> Now therefore, thus says the LORD of hosts, "Consider your ways!
>
> "You have sown much, but harvest little; you eat, but there is not enough to be satisfied; you drink, but there is not enough to become drunk; you put on clothing,

but no one is warm enough; and he who earns, earns wages to put into a purse with holes."

Thus says the LORD of hosts, "Consider your ways!

"Go up to the mountains, bring wood and rebuild the temple, that I may be pleased with it and be glorified," says the LORD.

"You look for much, but behold, it comes to little; when you bring it home, I blow it away. Why?" declares the LORD of hosts, "Because of My house which lies desolate, while each of you runs to his own house.

"Therefore, because of you the sky has withheld its dew, and the earth has withheld its produce.

"And I called for a drought on the land, on the mountains, on the grain, on the new wine, on the oil, on what the ground produces, on men, on cattle, and on all the labor of your hands" (Haggai 1:2-11).

"Will a man rob God? Yet you are robbing Me! But you say, 'How have we robbed Thee?' In tithes and offerings.

"You are cursed with a curse, for you are robbing Me, the whole nation of you!

"**Bring the whole tithe into the storehouse, so that there may be food in My house, and test Me now in this,**" says the LORD **of hosts, "if I will not open for you the windows of heaven, and pour out for you a blessing until it overflows.**

"**Then I will rebuke the devourer for you, so that it may not destroy the fruits of the ground; nor will your vine in the field cast its grapes,**" says the LORD **of hosts.**

"**And all the nations will call you blessed, for you shall be a delightful land,**" says the LORD **of hosts (Malachi 3:8-12).**

Another one of the words that the enemy has done his best to corrupt so that we cannot use it is "tithing." Like the other words he has directed his greatest powers of corruption toward, this word represents a truth that he knows will set us free from his yokes of bondage. Therefore I will use that word as much as I can without apology.

Tithing is the biblical term for giving the firstfruits of our labors to the Lord. It was specifically directed to be 10 percent and was practiced by the patriarchs before the Law of Moses was given. Abraham gave Melchizedek a tenth of the spoil he won in his battle with the kings, and Jacob also promised to give the

Lord a tenth of all that the Lord gave to him (see Genesis 14:20; 28:22). There were other offerings that one could make to the Lord, but this one was required.

Like most Christians, I have heard considerable teachings about tithing, both for and against. There are good arguments for and against it being a part of our New Covenant disciplines. Although I may not fully understand the theology of it, I have no doubt that it is a truth for all time and that God still honors it just as He promised in Malachi.

Tithing is not necessarily trying to live by the law, and it is not legalism, though it can be. There are people who pray legalistically, but does that mean that we should stop praying? I know people who witness, read their Bibles, and even worship under the compulsion of a religious spirit, but does that mean we should quit doing those things? Of course not. We may examine ourselves to be sure that we are doing them in the right spirit, but we must continue doing the fundamental disciplines of the faith. Giving the firstfruits to the Lord is one of those disciplines.

Giving the firstfruits of our income to the Lord in the right spirit is an act of faith. **"Without faith it is impossible to please Him, for he who comes to God must believe that He is, and that He is a rewarder of those who seek Him"** (Hebrews 11:6).

The Lord requires faith before He will release His power toward us. Giving our firstfruits to Him is an act of faith by which we are declaring that we trust Him as the Source of our provision.

The word of our testimony is one of the factors by which we overcome the world. I have the testimony that the only times I have suffered financially since becoming a Christian were when I neglected to tithe. This was usually done out of carelessness because I have always believed in tithing. However, every time I have suffered financial trouble and have gone back and checked my records, I found that my troubles began when I became careless in this one thing. When I repented and started giving the firstfruits of my income to the Lord again, the windows of heaven always quickly opened just as He promised.

When I became a successful businessman, I was giving large donations to churches and ministries. I was giving so much I started to just assume that I was giving at least ten percent, and I quit keeping up with it. At the very peak of my success, my business went into a tailspin and collapsed. Later, I felt compelled to go back and check my tithing record and found that my troubles began almost immediately when I started falling short in giving the first 10 percent to the Lord.

Over the years I have heard innumberable testimonies of dramatic turnarounds for people who committed themselves to tithing. When I taught this in our local church, I almost immediately started hearing testimonies of how financial difficulties began to turn around quickly for people after they became obedient in this. Without exception, the ones I have met who have chronic financial problems are also the ones who do not give their firstfruits faithfully to the Lord.

This does not mean that if you tithe this week, next week all your problems will be over. However, most people do almost immediately see the Lord begin to intervene and turn things around for them. I have witnessed many financial miracles, but sometimes the Lord intervenes by revealing other related strongholds that are hindering us. Regardless of how He does it, the end result of good biblical stewardship will be financial independence.

Good Intentions Are Not Obedience

I have watched quite a few people sink financially who did believe in tithing. Like I once foolishly did, they often said they were going to set aside their tithes until the Lord directed where to give them. This may sound noble, but if the money is still in our account, we have not given it. The Lord has already told us in His Word where to put it—in His storehouse, which is the church. Even if you do not agree with where your church leaders spend it, if you are a part of a local body, that is where your tithe should go.

I have heard others say that they do not tithe because everything they have is the Lord's. This is another tragic delusion. If everything they had was truly the Lord's, they certainly would be obeying His command to give the firstfruits. God does not need our money. The whole world is His. This is for us, not Him. Our excuses are only hurting us.

Since the church is the storehouse of God, does that mean that our congregations should tithe? Yes. First, it is a privilege, not a punishment. The Lord wants all of His people to be vessels through which His provision can flow to meet the needs He wants to meet. If we do not give, we cut off this flow. If you want proof that God honors the tithing principle with churches and ministries as well as with individuals, check the ones that are always struggling and those which always seem to have an abundance.

When we started our congregation we carelessly forgot to begin tithing from its income. The church suffered significant losses until we started to tithe from the church's income. Immediately the congregation's finances turned around. We could count these as coincidences, but we would have to be spiritually brain dead to do that.

When it was prophesied in the Book of Acts that a famine was going to come upon the whole earth, the churches did not begin to hoard; they took up an offering and gave! (see Acts 11:28-30) When we give, we are putting our treasures in heaven and our trust in God. If you believe that economic catastrophe is coming, the only wise place for you to invest is in the kingdom that cannot be shaken. You may think that you cannot afford to tithe, but you cannot afford not to. Most of us do not really need more income, we just need to have the devourer rebuked. But the Lord promises to do more than that; He promises that we will be so blessed that we will not have room enough to hold it all.

Are you that blessed? If not, then **"bring the whole tithe into the storehouse."** That means the before-taxes tithe. If we really believe the Word of God, why would we not want to bring the whole tithe and much more? He promises a blessing which is so great that we cannot even contain it anyway.

The following are a few other biblical promises that the Lord has given in relation to this. Knowing these and living by them can turn your whole financial life around. They are God's Word and He cannot lie.

"Give, and it will be given to you; good measure, pressed down, shaken together, running over, they will pour into your lap. For by your standard of measure it will be measured to you in return" (Luke 6:38).

He who gives to the poor will never want, but he who shuts his eyes will have many curses (Proverbs 28:27).

There is one who scatters, yet increases all the more, and there is one who withholds what is justly due, but it results only in want.

The generous man will be prosperous, and he who waters will himself be watered (Proverbs 11:24-25). *I Cor. 9:6-8*

Now this I say, he who sows sparingly shall also reap sparingly; and he who sows bountifully shall also reap bountifully.

Let each one do just as he has purposed in his heart; not grudgingly or under compulsion; for God loves a cheerful giver.

And God is able to make all grace abound to you, that always having all sufficiency in everything, you may have an abundance for every good deed (II Corinthians 9:6-8).

PART VII

Truth or Consequences

The Lord is going to judge the earth, and He is going to start with His own house. Judgments are not always condemnation, but they are the last call to repentance before the condemnation comes. It does not matter how much we attend church or how much truth we know. We will be judged by our *deeds* and by how we have lived. According to the Scriptures, to know the truth and not live it will only bring a more severe judgment.

Paul warned us to **"behold then the kindness and severity of God" (see Romans 11:22).** Many are deceived because they only see the kindness of God without also seeing His severity. Others are deceived because they only behold His severity but do not understand His kindness. To know the truth, we must see both His kindness and His severity together. *YES!*

Many presume that because we are now in the age of grace we can go on willfully sinning and God will overlook it. That is a most tragic delusion. We are in the age of grace *and truth* (see John 1:17). Our

57

God is a God of His Word. Our salvation depends on the fact that He keeps His Word. His people, who are called to be like Him, will also be a people who keep their word. Our yes is supposed to mean yes, and our no is supposed to mean no, without compromise.

To break our word to man is bad, but to break it with God could be the greatest human folly. Ananias and Sapphira bore the consequences of this, and Peter called it lying to the Holy Spirit. They wanted to be identified with the people who were giving everything, while they **"kept back some of the price" (see Acts 5:2)**. We would be much better off to never commit ourselves to being bondservants of Christ than to have made such a commitment and hold back part of the price. part of ourselves.

It is fundamental to the purpose of the church that we become a people of our word. The bridge that every relationship is built upon is trust. Without trust you can have forgiveness, and even love, but there can be no genuine relationship. The strength of the trust will determine the strength of every relationship. For the church to be the bridge-builder that helps restore the relationship between God and man we must be trustworthy.

The spirit of poverty gained major inroads into the church when some public ministries were caught in lies, unfaithfulness, or misusing the donations that were being given to them. By overreacting to this, many people stopped giving, which has caused serious repercussions in their lives. Many began to break their pledges to churches or ministries. Even ministries which were living by the highest standards of integrity were hurt, but the people who broke their pledges were hurt even more. To break a pledge is a serious matter, and the Scriptures make it clear that there are repercussions to this. Many are now suffering them.

Authority Has Responsibility

Because it is obvious that economics will be one of the major tests that all will be facing at the end of the age, it is imperative that if we are going to be a light in the darkness, we must live by much higher standards of integrity in financial matters. With authority comes responsibility. Adam was given authority over the earth and all of the beasts upon it. When he fell, everything under his domain suffered, including billions of people (see Genesis 1-3). When King David sinned by numbering the people, tens of thousands of those people died (see

II Samuel 24:1-17). We may say that this is not fair, but there could be no true authority if there were not also true responsibility. The more authority we have been given, the more those we have authority over will be hurt by our mistakes. These are God's children who are getting hurt.

The Scriptures exhort us, **"If we judged ourselves rightly, we should not be judged" (I Corinthians 11:31).** If we will examine ourselves, praying for the Lord to send His Holy Spirit to convict us of any evil way and embracing correction as a sign of God's favor, we will not have to endure the worse judgment when it comes. To serve the Lord's own household and to be stewards of His resources is a most serious matter. If we are called to do this, we must live by the very highest standards of integrity. We must understand the great responsibility we have been given and treat it with the seriousness that it deserves. It is not just the money that makes it serious, it is the integrity of His household.

Before the end, when nothing else on this earth is stable or trustworthy, the world will look at the church and see a people who can be utterly trusted, whose word is their bond, because the God they serve is trustworthy. The strength of our witness will be determined first by how much we trust God's Word and then by how much our word can be trusted. If we really believe God's Word, we will become like Him, and our words will also be true.

We must address these serious issues because we are coming to the most serious of times. There is a good fear; it is the fear of God. The lack of this pure and holy fear of God is possibly the main reason for the folly and delusion that the church has been trapped in for so long. There has never been a more serious business than our relationship with God. The judgment that will ultimately come upon the whole world is basically the result of the world treating Him so frivolously. Can we, who should know better than anyone, do that and expect to get away with it?

The God who loved us so much that He gave His only Son is not so harsh as to condemn us for petty mistakes. He knows the difficulties and pressures that we are subject to in this world. Although He knows that we will all stumble at times, the Scriptures are clear that presuming upon His grace and holding back when we have committed to give all will ultimately result in tragedy. It is not enough to know His Word; we must also keep it.

When Fear Is Freedom

When the storms come, it will be too late to try to build your house on the Rock. Let us now take heed to the Word of God that exhorts us to obedience:

Therefore, let everyone who is godly pray to Thee in a time when Thou mayest be found; surely in a flood of great waters they shall not reach him (Psalm 32:6).

Behold, the eye of the LORD is on those who fear Him, on those who hope for His lovingkindness,

to deliver their soul from death, and to keep them alive in famine (Psalm 33:18-19).

This poor man cried and the LORD heard him, and saved him out of all his troubles.

The angel of the LORD encamps around those who fear Him, and rescues them.

O taste and see that the LORD is good; how blessed is the man who takes refuge in Him!

O fear the LORD, you His saints; for to those who fear Him, there is no want.

The young lions do lack and suffer hunger; but they who seek the LORD shall not be in want of any good thing (Psalm 34:6-10).

The greatest promises in the Scriptures are to those who fear the Lord. Those who properly fear the Lord do not have to fear anything else on this earth. Those who know Him but do not properly fear Him have fallen to some of the greatest human tragedies. John was intimate with the Lord, while Judas was merely familiar with Him. There is a great difference. A familiarity with God that breeds presumption is possibly the most terrible delusion. However, familiarity that breeds an increasing revelation of just how awesome He is will inspire obedience.

To make a commitment to be a bond-servant of Christ and then go on living for ourselves would be a tragic folly. To know the truth and commit ourselves to live by it and then not do it is the very definition of a hypocrite, for which the Lord reserved His most vehement condemnation.

Even though we were bought with a price by the blood of the Lamb, He will not force us to serve Him. Obedience is required, but we must choose to obey because there is liberty not to obey. We may go years without suffering the consequences of our sins, but we will eventually reap what we sow. King Solomon stated in Ecclesiastes 8:11: **"Because the sentence against an evil deed is not executed quickly, therefore the hearts of the sons of men among them are given fully to do evil."**

When God does not swiftly judge our sin, it is often interpreted to mean that it does not matter to Him, but this is the delusion of a darkened heart. That He does not quickly discipline us is in itself a judgment that leads to further hardening.

We may then think that if the Lord would just execute His judgments quicker, we would not be prone to be so evil. This is true, but it would also inhibit the freedom that He gives us so that we can prove our devotion to Him. Who would ever disobey if they knew that swift judgment was coming? The same freedom that He gives us to disobey is the freedom that He gives us to obey and therefore prove our devotion. Those who love the truth will live by the truth even when it is not convenient or seemingly expedient.

PART VIII
Achieving Your Purpose

I was sitting in Reggie White's den listening to him and a teammate from the Green Bay Packers discuss their football careers. Some have called Reggie the best defensive lineman to ever play the game. He has been an All-Pro for ten straight years and was recently named to the All-Time NFL Team, which is composed of the best players over the seventy-five year history of the league. Shawn Jones, with whom Reggie and I were talking that day, has also been one of the outstanding players over the last decade.

During this conversation, it came up that there were probably many young men in every city who had the potential to be the very best NFL players. They have dreamed about doing it, yet they would never even play in an organized football game. Why?

What is true of those who have the potential to be great athletes but who never accomplish what they could is probably true of every position in life. Most of the potentially great musicians will spend their lives listening to others perform. The greatest potential businessmen, artists, scientists, statesmen, doctors, lawyers, writers, or ministers will probably spend their lives doing something that they are bored with and never do what they were given the talents to do.

Why? The answers are the same in almost every case. Understanding these reasons can make the difference between our having fruitful, fulfilling lives or ones filled with failure and frustration.

The Cause of Our Frustration

There will be frustration in our lives if we do not fulfill what we have been given the natural talents to do, but that frustration is even greater if we do not fulfill our spiritual destinies. This frustration could well be found at the root of many divisions in our churches, denominations, and even families. Frustration is already a major problem in the church, but the latter stages of this frustration, which are boredom and lukewarmness, can be even more devastating.

Being angry is not good, but it does show that at least one still has the ability to care. There is more hope for a congregation that has tensions in it than one that is asleep. However, if those in ministry are doing their primary job, which is to equip the saints to do the work of the ministry (see Ephesians 4:12), much of the energy that is now being manifested as tension will be used to produce fruit. And that is a primary reason why we are in this world.

"By this is My Father glorified, that you bear much fruit, and so prove to be My disciples."

"You did not choose Me, but I chose you, and appointed you, that you should go and bear fruit and that your fruit should remain, that whatever you ask of the Father in My name, He may give to you" (John 15:8,16).

According to the Lord's statement here, the primary purpose for which we have been called is to bear fruit that will remain. Bearing fruit is more than just growing personally in the fruit of the Spirit, as important as that is. The Lord is implying here that we are called to do something of such consequence that our lives will continue to impact this world even after we have departed. How many Christians do you know who are doing something with this potential? We might even ask: How many churches are doing this? They are few indeed. Yet this is the calling that is upon all of us. That is why the Lord placed in our hearts the desire to do something of significance. What is the difference between those who are bearing such fruit and those who are not?

All Christians have a ministry, a purpose that they have been given in this life. You were made for that ministry. The Scriptures state that you were even foreknown and called by God before the foundation of the world. Yet the Scriptures also teach that **"many are called, but few are chosen"**—going beyond calling to commissioning **(see Matthew 22:14)**. The first generation of Israel left Egypt and were called to go into the Promised Land, yet spent their lives wandering in circles in the wilderness—most people do the same thing. They spend their lives wandering in circles.

God does not want you to live in the perpetual frustration or boredom that comes from not walking in the purpose for which you were made. He wants you to live in a land **"flowing with milk and honey" (see Exodus 3:8)**, which is a land with much fruit. He wants you to have the indescribable pleasure of knowing that you have done His will—that you have accomplished all that He put you on this earth to accomplish. The first step to getting out of your wilderness is believing that He has something better for you and that He is able to bring you into it.

Many of the principles that make one an achiever in any field are the same that enable us to achieve our purposes in Christ. Because it is in the area of these general principles that most fail, these are the ones that we will focus on in this study.

There are five basic characteristics that can be seen in the lives of those who have accomplished notable achievements in this world. These same characteristics can be found throughout the Scriptures in the biographies of those who fulfilled the purpose of God in their generation:

1. They have a clear vision of their purpose.

2. They stay focused on their purpose.

3. They have the wisdom and resolve to gather the necessary resources or get the training required for accomplishing their purpose.

4. They do not associate with problem-oriented people but with solution-oriented people.

5. They refuse to let opposition stop them. They stay resolutely on the course, fulfilling their purpose regardless of setbacks or disappointments.

Now let's look at each of these in more depth as well as the stumbling blocks over which many fall and therefore fail to accomplish their purpose in this life.

Factor Number One: We Must Define Our Purpose.

It is improbable that we will fulfill our purpose if we do not know what it is. In the Scriptures, we can see that the Lord always reveals our callings before He expects us to accomplish them. He desires for each one of us to know our purpose in this life. Yet I have traveled extensively throughout the body of Christ and have found that only a very small percentage of believers even know what their personal callings are. Then only a small percentage of those are actually being equipped to fulfill them. This is obviously one of the most tragic failures of the church and the reason why she is presently having such a small impact on our world.

A primary reason why many do not know their calling is that they do not care enough to seek the Lord for it. He has ordained that we must ask, seek, and knock before we will receive. Our calling is possibly the most precious treasure that we have been entrusted with. Treasure is valuable because it is either rare or hard to find. Those who receive treasure too easily will not understand its true value. You may reply that the Lord showed the Apostle Paul his calling when he became a Christian, but by Paul's own confession he spent many years, often alone in the wilderness, defining that calling.

When you seek the Lord, get specific. *Those who have goals that are too general rarely accomplish them.* Those who want to "go into business for themselves" almost never do. Those who want to "be a musician" or "go into the ministry" almost never do; or if they do, they quickly fail. However, those who go into business because they love a certain product or service are much more likely to succeed. Those who fall in love with a certain musical instrument are much more likely to become musicians. Those who go into the ministry because they have a heart for reaching a certain people group with the gospel, planting churches, performing a certain ministry, etc., are much more likely to both do it and succeed.

Factor Number Two:
We Must Stay Focused On Our Goal.

This is truly a rare quality, and the lack of it removes many from the ranks of the achievers. The diversions can come from positive or negative factors. Many cannot see past the obstacles to attaining their goal, so they seek easier goals. Others are diverted by successes in lesser purposes. Harry Truman once remarked, "Most people are defeated by secondary successes." This is true.

One of the hardest tests that we must pass if we are going to fulfill our ultimate calling is to not be distracted by all of the other things that God is doing. God is doing many wonderful things today, but it is not possible for us to be involved in all of them. It is often difficult to resist joining another successful move of God, especially when well-meaning people often make others think that they are missing God if they do not join that movement. We must learn to give ourselves only to what God has called us to do. When we get before His judgment seat, He is not going to ask us how many successful churches or movements we were a part of—He is going to ask us if we did His will. YES!

Factor Number Three:
We Must Have the Wisdom and Resolve to Gather the Necessary Resources, or Training, for Accomplishing Our Purpose.

When we have a clear vision of our purpose and the resolve to stay focused on it, we are much more likely to see all that will be required for fulfilling it. For the fulfilling of every vision, there will be education, preparation, and training required. Between the time when God reveals the calling and the actual commissioning of that ministry, there will always be a time of preparation. The inability to understand this difference between the calling and the commissioning of God and the wise use of the time between them has caused the failure of many.

Albert Einstein once said, "Premature responsibility breeds superficiality." Martyn Lloyd-Jones once told R.T. Kendall that he thought premature success was one of the

Stay Focus/On Target God Wants You To Do!

most dangerous things that could happen to a person.

Paul was called as an apostle somewhere between eleven and thirteen years before he was commissioned to that ministry at Antioch (see Acts 13:1-4). He spent much of this time in the wilderness, seeking his own revelation of God's purpose in his life and a deeper understanding of the gospel he was to preach (see Galatians 1). He did not just sit back and wait—he used his time to prepare. This is where many fall short and therefore fail. Instead of being impatient, we should be thankful for all of the time that we are given to get ready for our calling, and we should use every bit of it wisely. This will be a primary factor that determines the quality and fruitfulness of our ministries.

Possibly the greatest difference between the star athletes, musicians, artists, or great professionals in any field and those who have the talents but are sitting on the sidelines is the devotion to training, practice, and preparation.

An ancient proverb states, "Those who fail to plan, plan to fail." There is a subtle mentality that has crept into large sections of the body of Christ that planning is not spiritual. Many actually infer that if you know what you are going to do ahead of time, God could not be in it. This is amazing because we are supposed to be taking on the nature of God, and this is profoundly contrary to His basic nature. In fact, the revealing of His plan is one of the most glorious revelations of His character. Jesus was crucified before the foundation of the world, and we were called in Him before the world began. That's planning!

If we are becoming like Him, planning should be one of our greatest skills. Rarely has anyone ever accomplished anything of significance without planning. It can be argued that the level of our ability to plan will be a major factor in determining the significance of our accomplishments. It is true that many who have the mentality that planning is contrary to the work of the Holy Spirit are overreacting to those who make plans according to mere human reasoning, plans which are often made without even consulting God. Even so, this overreaction and failure to properly plan has unquestionably been far more devastating to the church.

Factor Number Four: We Must Surround Ourselves with Solution-Oriented People.

One of the first steps that successful leaders implement when assuming a position is to get rid of everyone who spends more time talking about problems than about solutions. Is this not why the Lord Jesus Himself spent so much of His time developing the faith of those who would be His future leaders and why "**without faith it is impossible to please Him?**" (see Hebrews 11:6)

When General Grant took over the Union Army during the Civil War, it had already suffered many defeats at the hands of General Lee and the Confederate Army. The officers and men of the Union Army had become so conditioned to defeat that when Grant first marched against Lee, even members of his own command team prophesied his doom. These were promptly dismissed. Then, in his first engagement with Lee at the Battle of the Wilderness, reports came in from every division of his army that they were beaten. All day long his officers begged Grant to flee back to the safety of Washington before Lee cut them off from their path of retreat. Finally, when it was obvious even to Grant that they were beaten in that engagement, he astonished everyone by giving orders to turn south and advance on to Richmond.

When Grant's generals begged him to reconsider, thinking that he had gone mad, Grant dismissed them and retreated to the solitude of his own tent. He confided to a reporter that he had never been in a battle in which it did not look at some point like they were doomed, but he believed that in every crisis there was also an opportunity. When he pondered the fact that Lee would try to cut off his retreat north to Washington, he saw that it would actually enable him to do something that every other Union general had tried to do and failed—to get his army between Lee and Richmond so that he could advance on the Southern capitol. His "defeat" at the Battle of the Wilderness opened the door for his greatest opportunity, and he seized it.

When Lee heard that Grant had not retreated, but had rather continued his advance, he confided that the end of the Confederacy was near. When the Union troops started marching south, a great cheer went up from the entire army. For the first time they had a general who would fight. Lee would paste several more "defeats" on Grant, but never once did Grant consider retreating. Never once did he pay attention to the doomsayers. He probably never did win an outright battle against Lee, but he held his course until he won the war.

One of the basic principles that every successful leader understands is that if you are going to win and accomplish your goals, you must get rid of the people on your leadership team who are more focused on the problems than solutions. This is the principle of the ten spies at Kadesh-Barnea (see Numbers 13). The evil, negative report of these ten spies cost their entire generation their inheritance. If

CANNOT > CONVERT or CHANGE then, GET RID

you cannot convert or change such people on your staff or teams, you must remove them, or they will cost you the same.

Factor Number Five: We Must Refuse to Let Obstacles or Opposition Stop Us.

Some of the factors that have helped individuals attain extraordinary achievements in their lives can be controlled and some cannot. Those which can be controlled are such things as hard work, defining goals, staying focused on our goals, and attaining the necessary resources for achieving them. However, possibly the greatest single factor in releasing the highest levels of human achievement is one that we cannot control and usually will do everything that we can to avoid. That factor is *adversity.*

One of the faces of the Lord in Scripture is the face of an eagle. It has been said that all of nature fears storms except for the eagle. If a bird faces an opposing wind *at the proper angle,* it will be carried higher. Eagles learn this early and use such opposing winds to reach the greatest heights. The same is true of those who learn to soar spiritually. Every opposing wind is an opportunity to go higher, *if you will approach it at the proper angle* or *attitude.*

The primary delusion about accomplishment is the belief that what allows some to become achievers is the fact that they had favorable circumstances. Using this as an excuse is one of the main reasons many fail. The obstacles that confronted Reggie, Shawn, and almost every other player in the NFL were as great, or greater, than those facing others. They were not given special breaks. Very few achievers in any field are. In fact, when special breaks are given to those with great ability, it often works to cause them to fall short of fulfilling their true potential.

Alexander Solzhenitsyn once observed; "Even biology teaches us that perpetual well-being is not good for any creature." Adversity does more for our development than possibly any other single factor. Adversity helps us to focus, to eliminate the non-essentials, and to devote ourselves to the essentials. Adversity will cause the truly devoted to work harder, which will cause them to become stronger. If success comes too easily, we will become weaker.

This Is Not Magic

I have watched many of my friends who play golf try one new golf club or ball after another seeking the "magic remedy" that will improve their game. One famous golfer said in a commercial for a new golf ball, "This ball really can improve your game, if you will hit three hundred of them a day!" When the same golfer was once asked about a "lucky shot," he replied, "You know, the more I practice, the luckier I get."

The same is true of our gifts and callings. People frequently ask me to pray for them to have the same gift of writing that I have. To me that is almost like one of my student pilots asking me to pray for him to have the "gift of piloting" imparted to him. Would you fly with someone who received their "gift of piloting" that way? I don't think so. You would want them to have the best training and then thousands of hours of experience, too.

I do believe in prophetic impartation, but I think that very few people really understand it. Even spiritual gifts are imparted as seeds, which must be cultivated and cared for with great patience and devotion. Even spiritual gifts must be developed with training and experience, or we will be about as dangerous as the above student pilot. I would love to have the gift to just pray for people and command them, "Be mature!" That is one miracle that I cannot find anywhere in the Bible.

As was said of the Lord, to fulfill our purpose in this life, we must **"resolutely set [our] face to go to Jerusalem" (see Luke 9:51),** the place of our destiny.